CREATIVE RECIPES FOR

BISCUITS

a Salamander book

Published by Salamander Books Limited
LONDON • NEW YORK

Published by Salamander Books Ltd.,
129-137 York Way, London N7 9LG, United Kingdom.

ISBN 0 86101 614 9

Distributed by Hodder and Stoughton Services, PO Box 6, Mill Road, Dunton Green, Sevenoaks, Kent TN13 2XX.

CREDITS

RECIPES BY: *Pat Alburey, Carole Handslip, Lesley Mackley, Janice Murfitt and Louise Steele*

PHOTOGRAPHY BY: *Sue Atkinson, Paul Grater and Jon Stewart*

DESIGN BY: *Tim Scott*

TYPESET BY: *Maron Graphics, Wembley*

COLOUR SEPARATION BY: *P & W Graphics, Pte. Ltd.*

PRINTED IN BELGIUM BY: *Proost International Book Production, Turnhout, Belgium*

CONTENTS

ALMOND COFFEE SLICES

185 g (6 oz/1½ cups) plain flour
60 g (2 oz/¼ cup) caster sugar
3 teaspoons instant coffee granules
125 g (4 oz) unsalted butter
30 g (1 oz/¼ cup) ground almonds
little beaten egg to glaze
30 g (1 oz/¼ cup) flaked almonds
3 teaspoons granulated sugar

Preheat oven to 180C (350F/Gas 4). Grease a 28 x 18 cm (11 x 7 in) Swiss roll tin.

Sift flour into a bowl; stir in caster sugar and coffee granules. Rub in butter until mixture forms a light dough; work in ground almonds towards the end. Press dough into prepared tin. Brush surface with beaten egg and sprinkle evenly with flaked almonds and granulated sugar. Bake in the oven for 20 minutes or until golden brown.

Leave to cool in the tin for 10 minutes. Cut into 18 fingers and transfer to a wire rack to cool completely. *Makes 18*

Hazelnut Chocolate Crescents

250 g (8 oz) unsalted butter
90 g (3 oz / 1/3 cup) caster sugar
1 egg yolk
1 teaspoon rum
125 g (4 oz / 2 cups) blanched hazelnuts, ground
250 g (8 oz / 2 cups) plain flour
60 g (2 oz / 1/2 cup) cornflour
15 g (1/2 oz / 2 tablespoons cocoa powder
90 g (3 oz / 1/3 cup) icing sugar, sifted, to decorate

Preheat oven to 180C (350F/Gas 4). Grease several baking sheets.

In a bowl, cream together butter and caster sugar until pale and fluffy. Beat in egg yolk and rum. Stir in ground hazelnuts. Sift flour, cornflour and cocoa powder together over mixture. Stir in the dry ingredients, adding a little more flour, if necessary, to make a firm dough.

With lightly floured hands, break off walnut-sized pieces of dough and roll each into a 7.5 cm (3 in) length, tapering into pointed ends. Shape into crescents and place on prepared baking sheets. Bake in the oven for 20-25 minutes until firm. Transfer to wire racks to cool.

Gently toss biscuits in sifted icing sugar to coat completely. *Makes 40*

TURKISH SHORTBREAD BRACELETS

60 g (2 oz/⅔ cup) walnut halves, coarsely ground
125 g (4 oz) unsalted butter
30 g (1 oz/2 tablespoons) caster sugar
1 small egg yolk
2½ teaspoons strong coffee
1½ teaspoons brandy
30 g (1 oz/¼ cup) cornflour, sifted
155 g (5 oz/1¼ cups) plain flour, sifted
1-2 tablespoons strong coffee
125 g (4 oz/¾ cup) icing sugar, sifted

Preheat oven to 160C (325F/Gas 3). In a bowl, beat together butter and caster sugar until light and fluffy. Gradually add egg yolk, coffee and brandy. Stir in ground walnuts, cornflour and flour, to make a firm, soft dough; knead lightly.

On a lightly floured surface, divide dough into 16 pieces and roll each piece into a ball, then into a 15 cm (7 in) rope. Form the rope into a circle, pressing ends together firmly. Place slightly apart on baking sheets and bake in the oven for 20 minutes, until firm. Transfer to a wire rack to cool.

Brush each biscuit lightly with coffee, then sprinkle with icing sugar until thickly coated. *Makes 16*

PEANUT BUTTER COOKIES

125 g (4 oz / ½ cup) soft tub margarine
140 g (4½ oz) crunchy peanut butter
125 g (4 oz / ½ cup) caster sugar
125 g (4 oz / ¾ cup) light soft brown sugar
1 large egg, beaten
185 g (6 oz / 1½ cups) plain flour
½ teaspoon baking powder
¾ teaspoon bicarbonate soda
good pinch of salt
½ teaspoon mixed spice
¼ teaspoon ground cinnamon
2 good pinches of freshly grated nutmeg
halved glacé cherries and blanched almonds, to decorate

In a bowl, beat margarine with peanut butter, sugars and egg until well combined. Sift flour with baking powder, bicarbonate of soda, salt and spices. Add to mixture and mix well. Divide into 25 and shape into balls. Place, spaced well apart, on greased baking sheets. Flatten to 5 cm (2 in) rounds. Decorate with cherries and blanched almonds. Chill for 30 minutes. Preheat oven 190C (375F/ Gas 5). Bake cookies in the oven for 10-12 minutes. Cool on baking sheets for 5 minutes, then cool completely on a wire rack. *Makes 25*

PECAN & CHOCOLATE CHIP COOKIES

125 g (4 oz) unsalted butter
60 g (2 oz / ¼ cup) granulated sugar
60 g (2 oz / ⅓ cup) light soft brown sugar
1 egg
few drops vanilla essence
125 g (4 oz / 1 cup) plain flour
15 g (½ oz / 2 tablespoons) cocoa powder
½ teaspoon bicarbonate of soda
125 g (4 oz) plain (dark) chocolate chips
60 g (2 oz / ½ cup) pecan nuts, roughly chopped

Preheat oven to 180C (350F/Gas 4). Grease 2 or 3 baking sheets.

In a bowl, cream butter and sugars together until light and fluffy. In another bowl, beat egg and vanilla essence together; gradually beat into creamed mixture. Sift flour, cocoa and bicarbonate of soda over creamed mixture; stir in carefully. Stir in chocolate chips and pecan nuts.

Drop teaspoons of mixture, well apart, on prepared baking sheets and bake in the oven for 10-15 minutes or until mixture has spread and cookies are beginning to feel firm. Carefully transfer to wire racks to cool and become crisp. Store in an airtight container. *Makes about 28*

COFFEE MACAROONS

2 egg whites
125 g (4 oz / ½ cup) caster sugar
125 g (4 oz / 1¼ cups) ground almonds, sifted
3 teaspoons ground rice
3 teaspoons instant coffee powder
90 g (3 oz) plain (dark) chocolate, in pieces, to decorate

Preheat oven to 150C (300F/Gas 2). Line several baking sheets with rice paper.

In a bowl, whisk egg whites until soft peaks form.

In a second bowl, mix together sugar, ground almonds, ground rice and coffee powder. Carefully fold into egg whites, then mix well, until smooth. Roll into 18 balls, each the size of a small walnut. Put on prepared baking sheets and press lightly, to flatten. Bake in the oven for 25-30 minutes, until golden. Leave to cool on baking sheets. When cold tear away surplus rice paper from around each macaroon.

To decorate, melt chocolate in a bowl placed over a pan of hot water; stir until smooth. Spread chocolate over half of the top of each macaroon. Leave to set. *Makes 18*

CANNOLI

185 g (6 oz / 1½ cups) plain flour
30 g (1 oz / 2 tablespoons) icing sugar
30 g (1 oz) unsalted butter
6 teaspoons sweet sherry
6 teaspoons strong black coffee
oil for deep-frying
315 g (10 oz) mascarpone cheese
60 g (2 oz / ⅓ cup) icing sugar, sifted
30 g (1 oz / ¼ cup) chopped pistachio nuts
60 g (2 oz / ⅓ cup) chopped glacé fruits
sifted icing sugar, to decorate

To make pastry, sift flour and icing sugar into a bowl, rub in butter, then stir in sherry and coffee.

Mix to a firm dough, knead lightly, cover and chill for 30 minutes. On a lightly floured surface, roll out pastry thinly. Cut out fourteen 9 cm (3½ in) squares. Lightly grease several cream horn moulds. Wrap a square of pastry round each mould, forming a cone. Seal edges with water. Deep-fry 3 or 4 cannoli at a time on the moulds for 1-2 minutes, until crisp and golden. Drain on kitchen paper. Remove from the moulds and cool. In a bowl, beat together mascarpone, icing sugar, nuts and glacé fruits. Fill cannoli. Dust with icing sugar. *Makes 14*

VIENNESE BISCUITS

140 g (4½ oz/1⅛ cups) plain flour
15 g (½ oz/2 tablespoons) cocoa powder
125 g (4 oz) unsalted butter, softened
60 g (2 oz/⅓ cup) icing sugar, sifted
100 g (3½ oz) plain (dark) chocolate, melted
60 g (2 oz) unsalted butter
200 g (6½ oz/1 cup) icing sugar, sifted
2 teaspoons coffee essence
2 teaspoons milk
icing sugar, to decorate

Preheat oven to 180C (350F/Gas 4). Grease 2 baking sheets. Sift flour and cocoa together. In a bowl, cream butter and icing sugar together until light and fluffy. Add flour and cocoa and work until a smooth piping consistency. Spoon into a piping bag fitted with a 2.5 cm (1 in) fluted nozzle. Pipe 6.5 cm (2½ in) lengths onto prepared baking sheets. Bake in the oven for 15 minutes until firm. Cool for a few minutes, then transfer to a wire rack to cool completely. Coat ends of each biscuit with melted chocolate. In a bowl beat butter with half the icing sugar until smooth. Add remaing icing sugar, coffee essence and milk; beat thoroughly. Sandwich biscuits together with icing. Sprinkle with icing sugar to serve. *Makes 15*

PINEAPPLE GINGER FLORENTINES

90 g (3 oz) unsalted butter or margarine
90 g (3 oz / 1/4 cup) golden syrup
30 g (1 oz / 1/4 cup) plain flour, sifted
30 g (1 oz) angelica, roughly chopped
30 g (1 oz / 1/4 cup) crystallized ginger, roughly chopped
60 g (2 oz / 1/2 cup) slivered almonds, roughly chopped
60 g (2 oz / 1/3 cup) glacé pineapple, roughly chopped
1 teaspoon lemon juice
125 g (4 oz) plain (dark) chocolate, melted

Preheat oven to 180C (350F/Gas 4). Line 2 baking sheets with non-stick paper.

Heat butter or margarine and syrup in a pan until melted, then stir in flour, angelica, ginger, almonds, pineapple and lemon juice. Put mounds of the mixture, the size of walnuts, well apart on prepared baking sheets and flatten with a fork. Bake in the oven for 8-10 minutes. Leave to cool for 1 minute, then transfer to a wire rack.

Spread chocolate over the base of each florentine. Put biscuits, chocolate side up, on a wire rack, and mark the chocolate into lines with a small palette knife. Leave until set. *Makes about 14*

CRÈME DE MENTHE BISCUITS

250 g (8 oz) plain (dark) chocolate
30 g (1 oz/6 teaspoons) butter
220 g (7 oz/2 cups) digestive biscuit crumbs
90 g (3 oz/¾ cup) plain cake crumbs
caster sugar for sprinkling
60 g (2 oz/¼ cup) unsalted butter
125 g (4 oz/¾ cup) icing sugar, sieved
2 teaspoons crème de menthe

Make filling first. Place butter in a bowl and beat with a wooden spoon until soft and smooth. Gradually beat in icing sugar and crème de menthe until light and fluffy. Break up chocolate and place in a bowl. Add butter and place over a saucepan of hand-hot water. Stir occasionally until melted. Add biscuit and cake crumbs and stir until evenly mixed and mixture forms a ball. Sprinkle a 25 cm (10 in) square of foil with caster sugar.

Roll out chocolate mixture on the foil to a 20 cm (8 in) square. Spread crème de menthe mixture evenly over chocolate square to within 1 cm (½ in) of edges. Roll up carefully into a neat roll using the foil to help. Wrap in foil and chill until firm. Cut into thin slices as and when required. *Makes 20 slices*

TRADITIONAL SHORTBREAD

125 g (4 oz/½ cup) butter
30 g (1 oz/5 teaspoons) caster sugar
155 g (5 oz/1¼ cups) plain flour
pinch of salt
30 g (1 oz/2 tablespoons) fine semolina
caster sugar, to decorate

In a bowl, beat butter with sugar until creamy. Sift flour and salt into bowl, then add semolina. Blend in with a spoon, then work by hand to form a soft dough.

Knead dough lightly on a floured surface until smooth. Roll out to a smooth round, about 15 cm (6 in) in diameter. Very lightly flour a 17.5 cm (7 in) shortbread mould. Place shortbread, smooth-side down, in mould. Press out to fit mould exactly. Carefully unmould shortbread onto a baking sheet. Refrigerate for 1 hour. Place on baking sheet, prick well with a fork, then pinch edge to decorate.

Preheat oven to 160C (325F/Gas 3). Bake shortbread in the oven for 35-40 minutes until cooked through. Immediately shortbread is removed from oven, sprinkle very lightly with caster sugar. Allow to cool on baking sheet for about 20 minutes, then very carefully remove to a wire rack. *Makes 1*

GINGERBREAD MEN

500 g (1 lb/4 cups) plain flour
pinch of salt
2 teaspoons ground ginger
1 teaspoon mixed spice
2 teaspoons bicarbonate of soda
125 g (4 oz/½ cup) butter
60 g (2 oz/⅓ cup) light soft brown sugar
60 g (2 oz/¼ cup) caster sugar
90 g (3 oz/¼ cup) black treacle
60 g (2 oz/2 tablespoons) golden syrup
1 egg, beaten

Preheat oven to 180C (350F/Gas 4). Butter several baking sheets. Sift dry ingredients into a bowl and make a well in centre. Put butter, sugars, treacle and syrup into a saucepan and stir over moderate heat until melted. Pour into flour. Add egg and mix to form a dough. On a floured surface, knead lightly until smooth. Roll out to 0.3 cm (⅛ in) thick. Using a gingerbread man cutter, cut out as many shapes as possible. Place on baking sheets. Bake in the oven for 20 minutes until lightly browned. Cool on baking sheets then remove to wire racks to cool completely. Traditionally, gingerbread men are left plain, but if desired they may be decorated with royal icing. *Makes 23-24*

AMARETTI

1 egg white
2 teaspoons Amaretto di Saronno
155 g (5 oz / 1⅓ cups) ground almonds
30 g (1 oz / ¼ cup) bitter almonds, blanched and finely ground
250 g (8 oz / 1½ cups) icing sugar, sifted
icing sugar, to decorate

Preheat oven to 180C (350F/Gas 4). Grease several baking sheets and line with non-stick paper. In a small bowl, very lightly whisk egg white and Amaretto together.

Put ground and bitter almonds and sugar into a large bowl, mix together and make a well in centre. Pour egg white into well, then mix to form a paste. Divide mixture into 36 equal pieces; roll each one into a ball. Place on prepared baking sheets. Bake in the oven for 15-20 minutes until only just lightly browned. Remove from oven; immediately sift evenly with icing sugar. Cool on baking sheets. *Makes 36*

ADVENT BISCUITS

155 g (5 oz/1¼ cups) plain flour
90 g (3 oz/⅓ cup) butter
30 g (1 oz/¼ cup) ground almonds
45 g (1½ oz/8 teaspoons) caster sugar
1 egg yolk
1 egg white
250 g (8 oz/1½ cups) icing sugar, sifted
red, green, yellow and black food colouring pens

Preheat oven to 180C (350F/Gas 4). Lightly flour 2 baking sheets. Sift flour into a bowl; rub in butter finely. Stir in ground almonds, sugar, egg yolk and enough cold water to form a soft dough. Knead dough on a lightly floured surface, roll out thinly and cut out 24 ovals using a 5.5 cm (2¼ in) cutter. Arrange on baking sheets and make a hole in top of each biscuit. Bake for 10-15 minutes until lightly browned at edges. Cool on wire rack. Place egg white in a bowl, stir in enough icing sugar to mix to a thick consistency. Beat until smooth and glossy. Cover surface of each biscuit evenly. Place on rack to dry. When dry and hard, use food colouring pens to number biscuits 1 to 24 and draw a design or message on each biscuit. Thread biscuits with ribbons. *Makes 24*

CHEESE STRAWS

250 g (8 oz/2 cups) plain flour
½ teaspoon salt
½ teaspoon cayenne pepper
½ teaspoon dry mustard
125 g (4 oz/½ cup) butter
125 g (4 oz/1 cup) grated Cheddar cheese
1 egg, beaten
4 teaspoons finely chopped red and yellow peppers
1 clove garlic, crushed
4 teaspoons chopped fresh basil and parsley

Preheat oven to 200C (400F/Gas 6). In a bowl, sift flour, salt, cayenne and mustard. Cut butter into pieces, add to bowl and rub in finely. Using a fork, stir in cheese and egg. Knead into a smooth dough. Divide into 4. Flavour one piece with peppers, one with garlic and one with herbs, kneading lightly. Roll out each piece to a strip measuring 10 cm (4 in) wide and 0.5 cm (¼ in) thick. Cut into 0.5 cm (¼ in) strips. Arrange in straight lines on greased baking sheets. Knead trimmings together, re-roll and cut out circles using a 5 cm (2 in) and 4.5 cm (1¾ in) plain cutter. Bake in the oven for 5-8 minutes until pale in colour. Cool on wire racks. Serve straws in bundles threaded through pastry rings. *Makes 100 straws plus rings*

CHEESE THINS

125 g (4 oz/1 cup) plain flour
½ teaspoon salt
½ teaspoon pepper
½ teaspoon dry mustard
125 g (4 oz/½ cup) butter
125 g (4 oz/1 cup) grated Cheddar cheese
4 teaspoons fine oatmeal
1 teaspoon cayenne pepper
1 egg white

Preheat oven to 220C (425F/Gas 7). Lightly butter 2 baking sheets. Sift flour, salt, pepper and mustard into a bowl. Cut butter into pieces, add to bowl and rub in finely until mixture begins to cling together. Using a fork, stir in cheese and mix to a soft dough. Knead on a lightly floured surface and roll out very thinly. Using a 2.5 cm (1 in) oval cutter, cut out 80 oval shapes. Arrange on baking sheets, spaced apart. Mix together oatmeal and cayenne. Brush each oval with egg white and sprinkle with oatmeal mixture. Bake in the oven for 5-6 minutes until pale in colour. Cool on baking sheets, then remove carefully with a palette knife. *Makes 80*

COCKTAIL BISCUITS

375 g (12 oz/3 cups) plain flour
½ teaspoon cayenne pepper
1 teaspoon dry mustard
185 g (6 oz/¾ cup) butter, diced
125 g (4 oz/1 cup) grated Cheddar cheese
1 egg, beaten
1 teaspoon sesame seeds and 1 teaspoon poppy seeds
1 teaspoon curry paste
2 teaspoons tomato purée

In a bowl, sift flour, cayenne and mustard. Add butter and rub in finely. Using a fork, stir in cheese and egg until mixture clings together. Knead to form a smooth dough. Cut pastry into 4. Knead sesame seeds into one piece and poppy seeds into another. Form both into 15 cm (6 in) rolls. Wrap separately in plastic wrap. Roll remaining 2 pieces of pastry into 20 × 15 cm (8 × 6 in) rectangles. Spread one piece with curry paste and the other with tomato purée. Roll up Swiss-roll fashion. Wrap in plastic wrap. Chill all the rolls until firm. Preheat oven to 200C (400F/Gas 6). Line several baking sheets with non-stick baking paper. Slice each roll thinly and place a little apart on sheets. Bake for 6-8 minutes. Cool, then transfer to wire racks. *Makes 96*

WATER BISCUITS

185 g (6 oz / 1½ cups) plain flour
½ teaspoon salt
1 teaspoon baking powder
45 g (1½ oz / 9 teaspoons) butter or lard
60 ml (2 fl oz / ¼ cup) water

Preheat oven to 180C (350F/Gas 4). Butter several baking sheets. Sift flour, salt and baking powder into a bowl. Rub in butter or lard until the mixture resembles fine breadcrumbs. Add water and mix to form a dough. Knead dough on a floured surface until smooth. Roll out very thinly. Prick well with a fork. Using an 8 cm (3½ in) plain round cutter, cut out rounds from dough. Place on baking sheets. Re-knead and re-roll trimmings: cut out more rounds. Continue until dough is used up to make 18-20 in total.

Bake in the oven for 15-20 minutes until well cooked and only slightly browned. Remove to wire racks to cool. Serve with cheese or pâté. *Makes 18-20*

SCOTTISH OATCAKES

125 g (4 oz/1 cup) fine oatmeal
½ teaspoon baking powder
pinch of salt
30 g (1 oz/6 teaspoons) butter
6 teaspoons boiling water

Put oatmeal, baking powder and salt into a bowl, then rub in butter until mixture resembles coarse breadcrumbs. Add boiling water, mix to form a dough and knead until smooth. Dough will be sticky at first, but when kneaded will become drier and smoother as oatmeal absorbs water. Roll out dough on surface sprinkled with oatmeal to a round a little larger than 20 cm (8 in). Using a plate as a guide, cut dough into a neat round. Cut round into 8 equal pieces to form neat triangles.

Heat a griddle over a moderate heat and grease very lightly. Place oatcakes on griddle and cook for 8-10 minutes until well cooked through and corners curl upwards. Cool on a wire rack. Serve with butter and marmalade. *Makes 8*